Sigmund Freud

by

Ralph STEADman

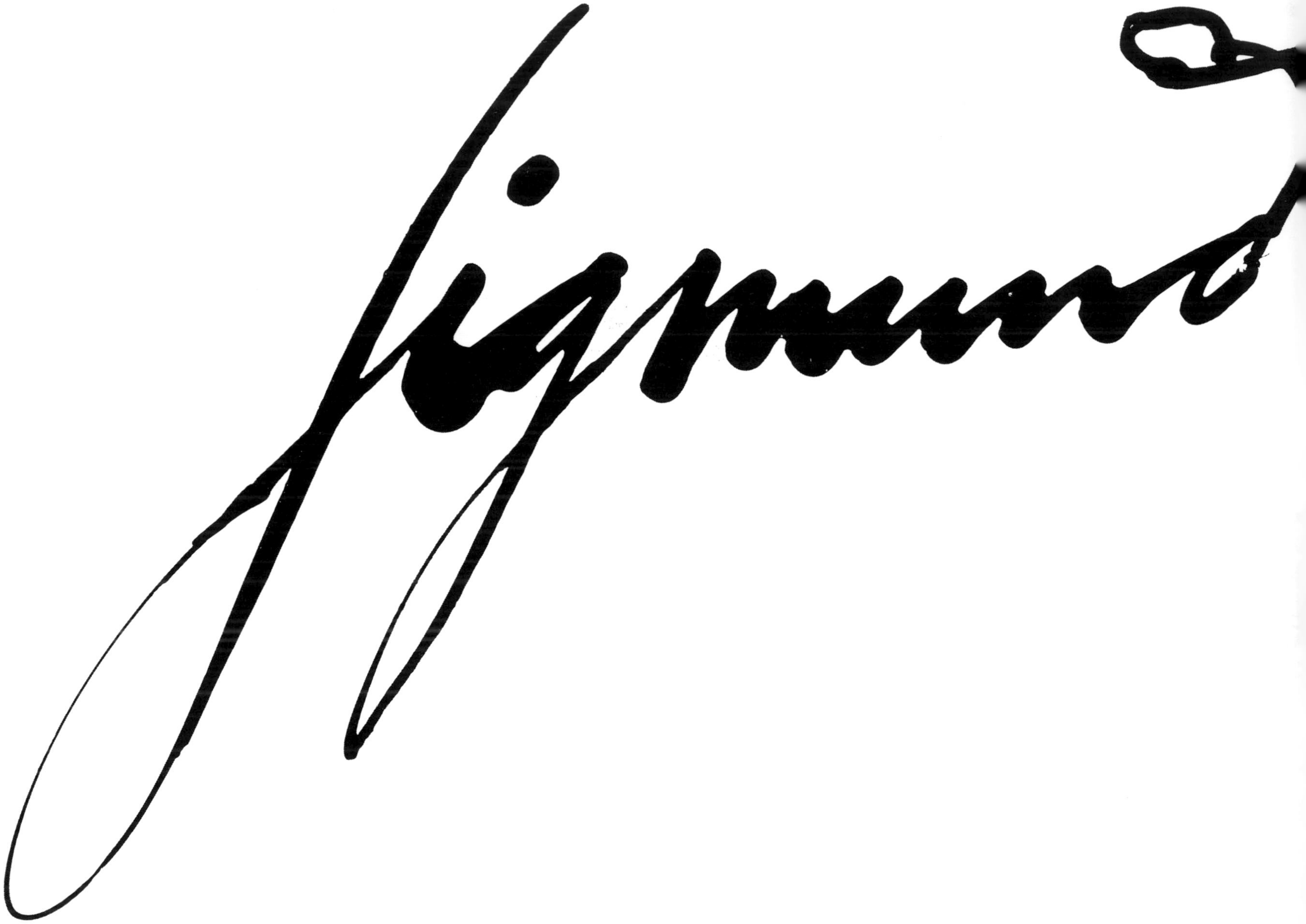
Sigmund

Freud

by

Ralph STEADman

FIREFLY BOOKS

A FIREFLY BOOK

Published by Firefly Books, 1997

Cataloguing in Publication Data

Steadman, Ralph
    Sigmund Freud

Includes index.
ISBN 1-55209-174-0

1. Freud, Sigmund, 1856-1939 - Caricatures and cartoons. 2. Freud, Sigmund, 1856-1939 - Humor.   3. English wit and humor, Pictorial.
I. Title.

BF109.F74S73 1997   150.19'52'092   C97-930853-4

Published by
Firefly Books Ltd.
3680 Victoria Park Avenue
Willowdale, Ontario
Canada M2H 3K1

Published in the U.S. by
Firefly Books (U.S.) Inc.
P.O. Box 1338, Ellicott Station
Buffalo, New York 14205

Printed and bound in Canada
by Friesens
Altona, Manitoba

For my Mother and Father

Goya's "Dream of Reason" could have been a piece of contemporary satire in Freud's Vienna. The tormented Viennese citizen hides his head in his hands, trying vainly to shut out the bats and demons of Freud's odious alchemy. As somebody once said, "Strauss taught the Viennese to forget; Freud forced them to remember."

Introduction

riting an introduction to a book about a genius like Freud in a nonacademic way and with humor in mind is a bit of a tightrope walk. If done either too seriously or too flippantly, the delicate balance is upset – so I'm in trouble already.

The work is done, but the front of any book sobs in its cups for lack of some introduction beyond a polite "How d'ya do." How to start? Was Freud amusing? A few jokes maybe. After all, it's supposed to be a book about Freud and humor. Memories? Evoke a period perhaps. Vienna just before the war. Darkness. Imagine . . .

A bitter March wind is no joke anywhere or at any time, especially when one is whistling down a long gaunt street rising steeply at its western end in the dreary ninth district of Vienna. The war clouds are looming and if you're walking down that street, keeping your thoughts to yourself as you try hard not to catch the eye of anyone in a "Heil Hitler" mob following a convoy of gray German tanks, it's even less of a joke.

Behind the doors of No. 19 Berggasse, Madame Freud was doing her valiant best to entertain a gang of armed Gestapo youths, too busy rifling the place as they searched for anti-Nazi documents to appreciate her housewifely overtures. Fearfully, she laid every last penny they had in the house on the table, 6,000 Austrian schillings in all (about $600). Then suddenly, disturbed by the commotion, Freud appeared at the door of his study. He glared at the intruders with eyes like an eagle, dimmed by age and the pain of a cancerous jaw, and declared:

"Help yourselves! It's more than I ever got for a single visit!"

Contrary to popular belief, Sigmund Freud did have a sense of humor—wry, dry and sometimes venomous – and it was never better than when he was under siege, which for the better part of his life he was. His contemporaries saw him as a humorless, frustrated tyrant, obsessed with sex, but I don't think he bothered to protest too much. Far better to acquiesce and conserve his energy for the real fight – that of gaining scientific verification of his ideas – than to play the red-nosed clown.

This book grew out of my desire to illustrate a series of classic Jewish jokes. Not long after, I discovered Freud's *Jokes and Their Relation to the Unconscious* (1905) and from then on there was no turning back. Having decided to illustrate the joking

Freud as Clown 1927

methods that Freud himself discussed and analyzed in this relatively little-known book, I watched the drawings grow – almost on their own – into a series about his life. I became intrigued with the notion that a drawing could convince an observer of its authenticity if what I drew contained enough reality from the known facts about his life.

There may be the odd wander in the guise of artistic license, but these are few and far between for I became a stickler for truth under Freud's influence. Even serious students of Freud may wallow in these pages, happy in the knowledge that neither the drawings nor the commentary will affect their objectivity, for all things checkable I checked.

As far as the development of the drawings is concerned, I allowed my mind to settle freely on any random detail of Freud's life and let things connect, partly in my mind and ultimately in the drawings, vaguely adopting the method of free association that was so fundamental to Freud's work. I did not dwell on Freud's own preoccupation with sex, feeling that by repressing it harshly, the drawings would be imbued with more electricity than they otherwise might have.

In fact, if you feel the need for some practice analysis, analyze my drawings. They must be loaded with unconscious symbolism.

You may not learn too much about the nature of joking from this book, but I shouldn't let that worry you. Providing you can still enjoy a good joke when you hear one, it seems a fairly painless way to learn a few things about one of the most magnificent thinkers this brow-beaten planet has ever produced.

Ralph STEADman
London 1979

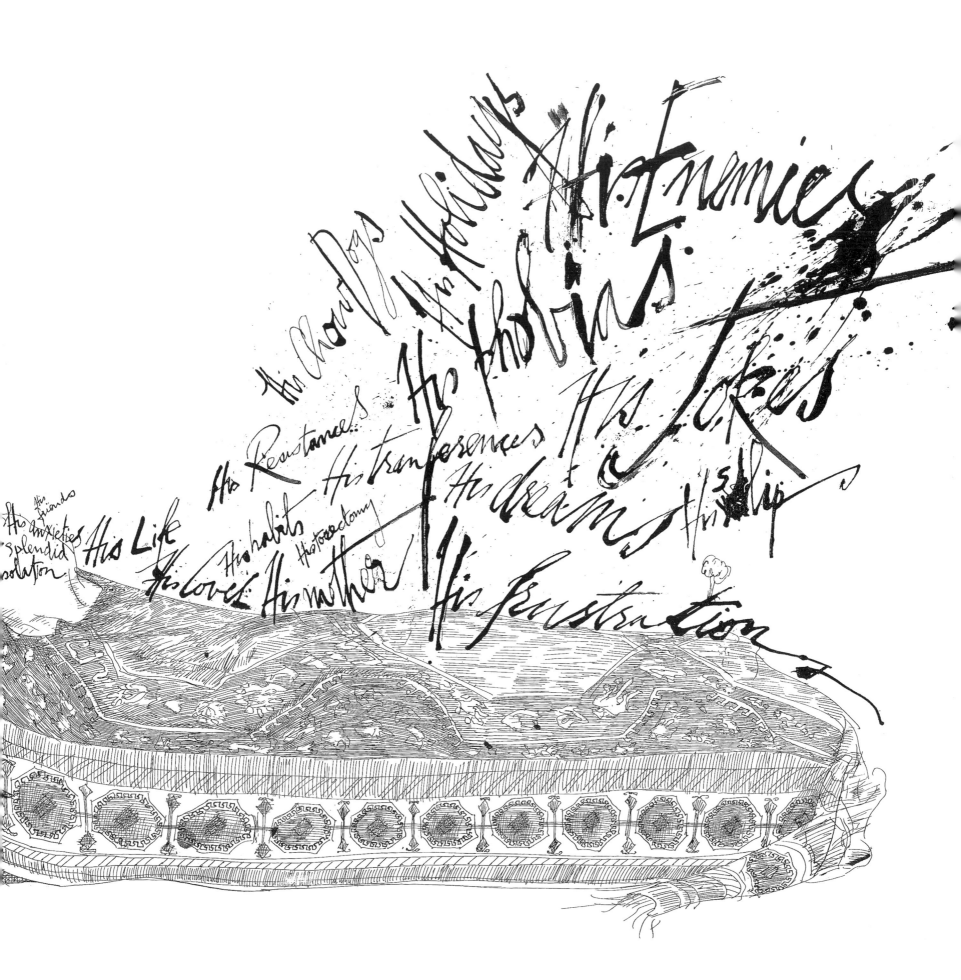

Freud listening to a joke told to him by
a colleague who has just learned of Freud's
intention to publish a paper on the Subject.

It was Freud's father who reproved him for bed wetting and other transgressions; not his mother, who was rather indulgent.

Thus, from a very early age, Freud came to see the father as the reality principle and the mother as the pleasure principle.

The eleven-month-old Freud was troubled by the birth of a brother named Julius, who divided his mother's love, giving Freud cause for jealousy and prompting him to think malevolent thoughts about his rival. When his brother died at only eight months, Freud was full of self-reproach.

Between the ages of 2 and 2½, Freud saw his mother naked and his libido was aroused. He also had a strong love-hate relationship with his older nephew John, son of his father's oldest son, Emmanuel, from a previous marriage. Matters were even further complicated when the disappearance of his nanny coincided with the birth of a new sister, Anna, dividing his mother's love yet again. (The nanny, incidentally, had been jailed for stealing.) Puzzled by the loss of the nanny and troubled by the appearance of yet another rival, the 2½-year-old Freud asked his other half-brother Philipp where the nanny had gone. Philipp jokingly replied that she had been locked in a wardrobe closet, which he duly led Freud to. When he flung open the door, there was, of course, no one inside and Freud, torn between spite and despair, burst into tears, demanding to see his mother as well as his nanny.

This incident serves as the inspiration for the drawing opposite, a visual projection of a **screen memory*** in which the adult Freud imagines himself standing before a chest, feeling that his mother – as well as his nanny – must be inside (a fear triggered by the fact that subconsciously he had noticed that his mother was not often with him at this time). In analyzing his own dreams from 1895 to 1899, Freud came to see any chest as a womb symbol and the opening of it as his fear that another brother or sister might emerge from his mother's womb.

Incidentally, the strange and threatening physical proportions of Freud's father in the drawing are an artist's daring attempt to visualize how the mature Freud, imagining himself as a child, would have seen

***Screen memory:** a memory which corresponds not to an event which actually happened, but to a fantasy of what in fact never happened. Imagine it to be an iceberg of which only a very insignificant tip shows up, the idea being that the spoken detail – no matter how small – is an indication of the much larger problem beneath the surface.

his father. If Freud were alive to verify the attempt, he might say:

"Gosh, that's just how I remember him!"
and this might well be a breakthrough in the history of speculative illustration.

Freud's father Jakob pursued a less and less lucrative career as a wool merchant and was constantly trying to meet mounting bills. One might see him as embodying the spirit of Mr. Micawber, who said:

"Annual income twenty pounds, annual expenditure nineteen nineteen six, result happiness. Annual income twenty pounds, annual expenditure twenty nought and six, result misery."

Had Jakob Freud muttered this remark, his son would have put it into the **unification** category of joking, according to the terms of reference that he himself developed in *Jokes and Their Relation to the Unconscious*. Three elements come into play in this particular joke: the annual income; the small difference between the amounts expended; and the world of difference between their effect, which unifies the whole and creates the wry joke. We are amused because we are made to realize the deeper philosophic relationship between the results.

Early on Freud developed a phobia of missing trains. As an adult, he would often march up and down along the platform one hour or more before his train arrived. He analyzed it all later and found that it was a fear of object loss – probably connected to his fear of losing his home and his mother's breast. On one of his first train rides, as the train passed through Breslau en route from Leipzig to Vienna, the three-year-old Freud saw gas flares burning for the first time.* The flares reminded him of the awesome tales of hellfire and damnation that his nanny used to tell him.

Freud (overleaf) is defending a window he wished to keep open on a train journey through Switzerland. He has just had to suffer a nasty piece of anti-Semitic invective:

"We Christians think of other people – you'd better think less of your precious self, mein Herr!"

This is a clumsy form of **tendentious joke.** The technique employed provides a joking envelope in which a purposeful remark is delivered via any of the joking varieties. The opposite of a tendentious joke is an **innocent joke,** which is made for the sake of the joke alone. These are often funnier when raised naturally in the course of related conversation and not in an endless stream, as often happens when somebody at a party fancies himself as one hell of a wag and sparks

*The train route from Leipzig to Vienna was fraught with difficulties for Freud. On the same journey a year later, he had occasion to see his mother naked (what again?). Forty years later he would relate the event to his friend Wilhelm Fliess in Latin.

off the whole room into an orgy of bubbling banality.

The tendentious joke satisfies more than the need for a pleasurable effect, as the originator – and often the hearer – receive the pleasure of the laughter as well as the intent, knowing that the laughter hastens the remark toward its target.

For instance, imagine that Freud greets an acerbic old acquaintance he has not seen for some time in a familiar way.

"Hello, Fritz. How are things?"

To which the gentleman, obviously sensitive about his name in the anti-Semitic climate of late-nineteenth-century Vienna, retorts:

"It's Friedrich, you cretinous Jew."

"Oh, really," replies Freud instantly. **"What does the 'U' stand for?"**

Regarding his unpleasant experience in the train, if Freud had not been so disarmed by the strength of the anti-Semitic crowd that surrounded him, he might have been able to turn the tables on his aggressor and pay him back in his own coin with a **unification joke** such as:

"Dear me, then. Isn't this the cattle train to Winterthur?"

In 1879, at the age of twenty-three, Freud spent twelve months in the army. As a child, he was passionately interested in the glories of great battles and the exploits of great commanders like Hannibal, Napoleon and Masséna. At the age of fourteen he meticulously followed the developments of the Franco-Prussian War, and at one stage he even had dreams of becoming a great general himself. However, his army experience, coming as it did right in the middle of his scientific studies* at the University of Vienna under Professor Brücke, stifled any further ambitions in that direction.

Anyone who has been within spit-and-polish distance of a parade ground will appreciate the painful relationship that exists between a professional soldier, whose rank is more the result of blind, dog-like loyalty than merit, and his victim, the debutant soldier who has the coordination reflexes of a newborn cow . . .

Only a moment ago Freud was facing in the opposite direction to the rest of his regiment:

"**Do you know what you are, laddie?**"

"**No, Sergeant.**"

"**You're a brainless idiot. *What* are you?**"

Not even Freud's overpowering intellect could help him here.

"**I'm a brainless idiot, Sergeant,**" he replied meekly.

"**Which is why, laddie, you don't know your left from your right. *What* don't you know?**"

"**I don't know my left from my right.**"

"**Right *what*, laddie?**"

"**Right hand?**"

"**Right, *Sergeant*, laddie. What did I say?**"

"**Right, Sergeant, laddie.**"

"***Wrong*, laddie. Right, *Sergeant*, Sergeant.**"

"**Right, Sergeant, Sergeant – Sergeant?**"

"**My God, you brainless cretin! Listen to me, laddie. I'm going to drill you until the sweat pours off you in drops of blood. Then I'm going to pack you up in a plain brown wrapper, laddie. And then, laddie, I'm going to send you to the enemy with a slow-burning fuse. *What* am I going to do, laddie?**"

"**I shudder to think, Sergeant. Do you mind if I sit down?**"

N.B.: As a proud British subject, I could not quite give up the notion of a sergeant-major always having a short stick, though strictly speaking an Austrian drill sergeant would never carry such a thing.

*Readers might be interested to know that even at this period Freud was marked for greatness. Quite by chance, in the course of his experiments during this period, he discovered the testes of an eel. He was in Trieste at the time.

Freud telling a young Lady of his Acquaintance a smutty joke & trying to explain why he had the compulsion to tell it.

Freud telling a young lady of his acquaintance an off-color joke and trying to explain why he had the compulsion to tell it. If we are discreet, we might perhaps overhear . . .

" – thought it would amuse you, that's all."

"Hmmmm, in what way?"

"Yes – well – if I try to *explain* the joke it won't seem very funny."

"Then why did you tell it?"

"No, what I mean is – if you don't get it right away, it won't help if I explain it."

"You are perspiring. Are you all right?"

"Yes, perfectly – it's rather warm in here – no, what I mean is, *why* I told it rather than *what* it means might be of interest."

"What?"

"The joke."

"Oh, that. I thought you already have."

"Well, I was about to."

"I do beg your pardon, do go on, Herr—er . . ."

"Freud. – Well, it's not easy, but, well, to be quite frank, Fräulein—er . . ."

"Morecock."

"Fräulein Morecock, when one tells a vulgar joke, it is usually because the teller is strongly attracted to the—er—hearer, and hopefully the—er—hearer usually becomes aroused or even excited in return, when realizing the teller's own excitement. But the obscenity, of course, is only tolerated when it has the character of a joke, particularly in polite society. Among country people, or in inns of the humbler sort, it will be noted that it is usually not until the barmaid, or the innkeeper's wife perhaps, enters the room that smuttiness starts up. Only at higher social levels, of course, is the opposite found, where the presence of a woman brings the smut to an end. Though occasionally, if the teller feels perhaps particularly aroused by the hearer, Fräulein—er—Morecock, usually a woman, he feels compelled to make this urge felt by the use of—er—suggestive words cloaked in a joking form. These words may then awaken in her some reciprocal signs of —er—passive exhibitionism – (She blushes.) If the reciprocation emerges quickly, then the smutty joking effects have no further use, for the result usually manifests itself in some—er—physical action between the two parties concerned. In short, the joke will have served its purpose. However, if the lady shows no signs at all of —er—pursuing the matter, there is no harm done and the teller can retreat, as it were, behind the excuse that it was only a joke, which becomes an aim in itself in the shape of—er—smut, pure and simple, even becoming hostile and cruel as it summons to its aid against the obstinate hearer the sadistic components of the—er—sexual instinct. The teller may also enlist the aid of a third person, usually another man, as a second hearer which will give the teller moral support and possibly further ease his embarrassment as the second hearer enjoys the—er—smutty joke's yield of—er—pleasure."

"Herr Freud, are you trying to seduce me?"

"Good heavens, Fräulein Morecock! I was merely—"

"What was the joke again?"

"The joke? What joke? Oh! Yes, er— A wife is like an umbrella, Fräulein Morecock. Sooner or later one takes a cab."
"I still don't get it."*

A week later Freud met Martha Bernays, the lady destined to become his wife.

For three years during the early 1880s Freud was desperately courting Martha Bernays. He kept alive the fire in his heart for her mainly by letters. These were his quixotic years, when his mind was full of desperate ideas struggling to emerge. Genius must do what it must, but not before its time; Freud's psyche was still, as yet, a battleground full of warring generals with no soldiers to carry out their commands.

Here the love-lorn Freud struggles to express his deep love for Martha, but to avoid hypocrisy he feels compelled to write about what is uppermost in his mind. What shall it be? A futile attempt to explain his work on the chemical treatment of brain tissue samples? Or perhaps he ought to describe an illustration from *Don Quixote*, showing how a wretched little knight has cut in half six giants with one blow of his sword? In his imagination he would have identified with the wretched little knight and seen his father as one of the giants. Having disposed of all obstacles, he would then dash off to rescue a damsel in distress and carry her away with him to the pinnacles of scientific achievement. But, alas, he would hear her say in his moment of glory:

"If it's going to be a long ride, would you mind taking your sword off?"

This is a **double meaning with allusion joke** – the double meaning alluding to the doubts brought on by long periods of loneliness and sexual privation. More precisely, Freud would have called this a **double entendre** because the effect of the joke depends quite specifically on sexual innuendo. The funniest jokes of all, he declared in *Jokes and Their Relation to the Unconscious*, are often subtle allusions to cruder themes based on reference to forbidden subjects, which is why sex jokes (as in the previous dubious example) are the most popular of all, particularly in mixed company.

In other words, a sex joke enables you to state a hidden wish to members of the opposite sex without sounding blatantly disgusting... or positively perverted!

*For those of you who don't understand the joke either, Freud explained it this way:
... a bewildering and apparently impossible simile, [which] may be worked out as follows. One marries in order to protect oneself against the temptations of sensuality, but it turns out nevertheless that marriage does not allow of the satisfaction of needs that are somewhat stronger than usual. In just the same way, one takes an umbrella with which to protect oneself from the rain and nevertheless gets wet in the rain. In both cases one must look around for a stronger protection: in the latter case one must take a public vehicle, and in the former a woman who is accessible in return for money.

Freud arrives in Paris on the Hamburg train in 1885 to study neurology under the great master Charcot at the Salpetrière. His railway phobia could not have helped his nervous state very much. Nor could the remark of a porter who, having been brusquely refused permission to carry Freud's suitcase on account of Freud's precarious financial state, retorted:

"Il y a quelqu'un comme vous dans tous les trains."*

Precisely which of Freud's characteristics the porter was referring to is not made clear for he does not in any way qualify the remark. But we can immediately conjure up in our minds an abstract image of the characteristics the porter may be alluding to. We form an **analogy** (see page 47) of what we think he means, and we invariably smile, even though Freud did not consider analogies as one of the true categories of joke techniques. A nonspecific character assessment fills the space left in our minds by the porter's omission of what he is alluding to. An entire life history is created by observing the spirit of his remark – a life history which cannot possibly be based on fact, but only on the quality of our assessment. If the porter had offered his services to the man walking directly behind Freud, say, the same remark would probably have elicited from us an entirely different response.

What the porter could not possibly have known, of course, was that he was addressing a budding genius – a man who belongs to a handful of men throughout history destined to change our fundamental vision of the world, a man whose very name evokes an entire world of meaning . . .

And there certainly wasn't one of *those* on every train.

In this particular situation, we, as observers with hindsight, can view the incident and enjoy the remark as an unconscious historical overstatement. Our first inclination is to agree with the porter with an overenthusiastic "Yes" or "You're telling me." But within moments we must surely reassess our opinion and disagree with him. Between these two

*Trans. "There's one like you on every train.

responses, the remark has changed from an **analogy without qualification** into what Freud would have referred to as **representation by the opposite,** which is only destined to be so in light of subsequent events.

Freud in Paris at the Salpetrière, observing the effects of hypnosis on hysterics in Charcot's class in 1885-6.

Although Freud's psychological theories began with Charcot and Breuer, the principles he based them on (but found himself peculiarly at odds with later in life) in fact go back to his student days under Professor Brücke, director of the Physiological Institute at the University of Vienna. Brücke's ideas were tied to the beliefs of a far-reaching scientific movement founded and dominated by Hermann Helmholtz and Brücke. The ideas of this Teutonic group of scientists permeated the consciousness of German physiologists and medical men in the mid-nineteenth century. They believed that the brain and the nervous system were responsible for their own malfunctions and those of all other parts of the body. When Freud eventually challenged this view by claiming that something as intangible as the mind could also be the cause of bodily disturbance, he was looked upon by the entire Helmholtz school as not only a heretic but a fool.

Before Charcot, hysteria was considered to be merely a form of simulation or at best hypochondria. A symptom mainly found in women, it was believed to be a disorder of the womb which could be treated either by extirpation of the uterus or by driving the displaced womb back into place with the use of valerian, a variety of herb that smelled not unlike sweaty feet, which the womb naturally disliked.*

But Charcot's work changed all this. Overnight hysteria became a respectable disease of the ner-

*It has been said that a Herr Professor R. Idris Steadmann (no relation), writing at this time, challenged the orthodox notions of the Helmholtz school by arguing that hysteria in women is not always caused by the repression of their sexual urges or indeed their distaste when they discover their own preoccupation with the subject. He apparently cited several cases documenting that it was not uncommon for a woman with a record of staggering and varied sexual activity to have hysterics at the mere sight of the naked form of a potential lover whose physique in all its parts was less than substantial.

Ralph STEADMAN

vous system, for the great neurologist had established it within the parameters of the Helmholtz school.

To Freud's discomfort he found himself identifying with Charcot's patients. He, too, had sensed in himself hysterical symptoms probably induced by long periods of thwarted sexuality. In 1895 he wrote:

"Every hysteria is founded in repression, always with a sexual content."

This was no joke at all to Freud, but it did help to form the basis of his own self-analysis, which ultimately led to the discovery of psychoanalysis.

For a few years Freud suffered from occasional depressions and apathy brought on, in part, by long periods of not seeing his loved one, Martha Bernays. It was many years before he was able to dispel these anxieties through self-analysis.

In 1884 he developed an interest in the physiological action of cocaine in the hope that he might perhaps discover something important and make a name for himself, which would enable him to marry Martha a year or two earlier than he had ever dared to expect. He experimented on himself and found that not only did the drug miraculously lift his depression, but it also restored his energy and vigor. It was a colleague, Carl Koller, who eventually took the praise for discovering the most beneficial use of cocaine – as an anaesthetic in eye surgery – but Freud up to this time had found it a wonderful drug to take for anything from diabetes and migraine to heartburn and piles. He sent some to Martha to make her, as he put it, "strong and give her cheeks a red color."

Freud took cocaine himself just before seeing Martha for the first time in months in an effort to demonstrate to her:

"Who is the stronger: a gentle little girl who doesn't eat enough; or a big, wild man who has cocaine in his body?!"

One can only hazard a guess at what

30

Martha would be anticipating in her mind of the man who had written so copiously and passionately during their interminable separation. Surely she could not have expected the figure who leapt out at her from behind the curtains! Freud's behavior must surely have been forged by a potent combination of the bottled-up force of unrequited love, sexual repression and a highly exhilarating dose of cocaine.

And if he said:

"My darling, it's been so long!"

. . . one must forgive him the transgression. Freud himself would have classified the remark a **double entendre,** where the effect of the joke has a quite explicit sexual meaning, which at the time Freud was completely unaware of since the remark had thrust itself up from his unconscious.

An evening in the Prater. Two men are sitting at a café discussing music and musicians. One is championing the work of a modern young composer in glowing terms:

"His music will be played when Beethoven and Strauss are forgotten."

The other replies nonchalantly:

"Hmmm, and not until!"

Rather than bothering to argue that his friend's opinion may not be the case, the man appears to agree. He has used a technique of joking which Freud called **representation by the opposite** – a technique that demonstrates a certain irony (see page 85).

The real irony here is that Freud did not overhear the joke. At the time, he was idly rocking to and fro in a swingboat on the Big Wheel, trying to make himself giddy in order to test the effect of cocaine on seasickness.

N.B., for sticklers of detail: Owing to the artist's reluctance to repeat himself, only half the swingboats that existed on the Big Wheel at this time are actually shown in the drawing. Some of the swingboats were subsequently damaged by bombs during World War II, but if you prefer, blame it on the brain-damaged artist and his lack of knowledge of perspective.

Both Freud and Josef Breuer had been subjected to the advances of sexually aroused female patients who had flung their arms around them during treatment. Unlike Freud, however, Breuer was full of self-reproach after one such experience and tried desperately to repress it because he viewed the incident as the result of some personal indiscretion on his part. He interpreted his own warmth and compassion toward his patients as a seduction. His need to be liked and his own impulse to reciprocate shocked him and he recoiled, even though he knew secretly that it was what he really wanted.

Only because of Freud's resistant–oops, Freudian slip!–rather, *persistent* interest in the case of "Anna O"* and his own unexpected experience with one of his own patients did he get Breuer to admit to the very same experience – and not without a certain relief on Breuer's part! Nevertheless, Breuer fought shy of any connection between these experiences and what their observations had brought to light. Namely that (as I understand it): a phenomenon occurred during prolonged hypnotic treatment whereby a patient, by talking out the events of the day, would, as it were, sweep the mind of any disagreeable events and, as treatment progressed, would develop a strong attraction – and, much to Breuer's dismay, an erotic attraction – to the person treating them.

The phenomenon was to become the fundamental effect necessary to break down resistances within patients so that they could recall and relate unpleasant early experiences, or traumas, which Freud found remarkably often to be of a sexual nature. It was Breuer's reticence to take a stand and talk about sex publicly, for fear of becoming an outcast, that ultimately precipitated a bitter break in Freud's and Breuer's relations.

Here we find Freud entering Breuer's consulting room at the suggestion of Breuer's wife Matilde, only to find Breuer in the clutches of a patient.

"**Josef,**" says Freud, "**that's the third time this week! Either your technique is improving, or you've changed your toilet water!**"

This is an **overstatement joke with an allusion by means of omission.** Freud has overstated a repressed fact to create a joke, which diffuses the embarrassment in the room. The allusion by means of omission comes into play because Freud has omitted to refer to the slight odor which Breuer emitted (and don't we all!) when he was confronted by the incident, which he wished would go away.

*"Anna O," whose real name was Bertha Pappenheim, was a patient of Breuer's who displayed, among other things, a split personality. She would move from one identity to the other in a state of auto-hypnosis from which she would emerge clear and normal – or, conversely, strange and unpredictable! She was emerging from just such a state one day when Breuer arrived to treat her and, to her great relief, she began to relate all the unpleasant occurrences of the day. Ernest Jones, Freud's biographer, writes that it is she who must be credited with prompting the discovery of what became known as the **talking cure,** one of the fundamental processes of psychoanalysis. Anna O herself referred to Breuer's cathartic method of treatment as a kind of "chimney sweeping" of the mind. It is only in retrospect that one can see Anna O's sublimated desire that Breuer himself should sweep *her* chimney.

Bertha Pappenheim remained unmarried and was later to distinguish herself as one of the earliest fighters for women's rights.

reud stands transfixed listening to a brisk interchange triggered off by the suggestive remark:

"I didn't know your Grete was married!"

To which Grete's grandmother replied:

"I've told the Rabbi, if only you men wore your trousers the same way round some of you wear your collars, this would never have happened" – thus providing Freud with a perfect **double entendre.**

ot ve have here is a situation for a **displacement joke** – the essence of which lies in the joke's ability to divide our train of thought.

A horse dealer could have sold the man in the foreground his horse with the following sales pitch:

"If you get on this horse at four in the morning, you can be in Vienna by half past six."

To which the man could have replied quite rightly, and perhaps with a twinkle in his eye:

"What should I be doing in Vienna at 6.30 in the morning?" – thus creating a division of one's train of thought, an unexpected twist.

In September 1899 Freud finished the last chapter of *The Inter-pretation of Dreams* in an arbor at Berchtesgaden in Bavaria, where his family often spent their summer holidays. The chapter, describing the psychology of dream processes, is perhaps the most difficult and abstract of all his writings. Since July 24, 1895, when he made the first complete analysis of one of his dreams (known as Irma's Injection) at the Schloss Bellevue near Vienna and, in turn, realized that the fulfillment of a hidden wish is the essence of a dream, he had been obsessed by the implications of his great discovery. He wrote at great length about it to his friend Wilhelm Fliess, who complained at the time that there were too many jokes in dreams to give them any serious scientific significance. However, in spite of this (and not in small part because of it), Freud continued to give the subject his full attention.

His daughter, Anna, then only four and a half years old, has been watching her father intently for some time.

Freud looks up and says: **"Anna, my love, what are you thinking?"**

Anna replies: **"The fly on your head has been there an awfully long time."**

"Probably," says her father smiling, **"but not as long as the fly inside my head."**

"Then that must be the same one, Daddy, because it came out of your ear."

Though Anna had obviously not understood her father's remark, they had just made a joke from a subspecies of indirect representation which Freud called **representation by something small or very small,** which performs the task of giving full expression to a whole characteristic by means of a tiny detail – a characteristic mechanism, incidentally, displayed by obsessional neurotics.

N.B.: Serious students of Freud will no doubt realize that the building situated directly below the uppermost hyperdermic needle in the drawing is the Schloss Bellevue itself, where Freud mused that perhaps some day there would be a tablet bearing the following inscription:

In this house on July 25th, 1895. the secret of dreams was revealed to Dr. Sigmund Freud.

Albert Einstein emerges from a bath-house and overhears one Jew greeting another before entering:

"So, Moshe, another year gone by already!"

Einstein recalled the joke years later when he and Freud met in Berlin over Christmas of 1926. ("He is cheerful, sure of himself and agreeable," wrote Freud jokingly soon after the meeting. "He understands as much about psychology as I do about physics, so we had a very pleasant talk.")

Freud categorized the bath-house joke as an **allusion by means of omission joke;** i.e., the train of thought leading to the allusion – that in general practice most people, even Jews, take more than one bath a year – is omitted.

N.B.: Experts might date this picture about 1900 somewhere in West Germany, probably Ulm, but it is more likely the ghetto in Cracow, where many emigrant Jews set up shop. The only puzzling factor is the appearance of Einstein (second from left), for in 1900 he was only twenty-one. People who knew him, however, said he looked old for his age.

Wilhelm Fliess, Freud's very close friend for thirteen years, accuses him of being left-handed. Freud transfers his cigar back to his right hand, turns to Fliess and replies:

"As far as I recall, in my childhood I actually had two left hands, but the one on the right always took preference!"

He had created an **overstatement joke.** This type of joke is similar in character to **representation by the opposite,** due to the fact that the expected answer of agreement is displaced by an intensified "No" – i.e., an exaggerated denial functions in much the same way as an overstated affirmation.

This was their last meeting – or congress*, as it was then called – in Achensee in the summer of 1900. Wilhelm Fliess, a nose and throat specialist, harbored a theory that the nose swelled during genital excitement and menstruation. He also claimed that all neurotic manifestations and, indeed, most bodily functions were determined by periodic laws (connected with the numbers 23 and 28). This being so, he considered all of Freud's findings to be *de facto* irrelevant and meaningless, even if correct. Fliess called Freud "a mere thought reader."

Freud had his own thoughts on the matter and his reaction here represents a strong physical overstatement of his opinion.

*Congress: in German, a euphemistic term meaning sexual intercourse, in common use at the turn of the century.

Rome, late in the summer of 1901. The city had always meant two conflicting things to Freud: it was the Rome of Antiquity whose culture deeply interested him, the culture which gave birth to European civilization; and it was the Christian Rome, which destroyed and supplanted the older Rome. The Christian Rome could only be an enemy to him, for he had always seen it as the source of anti-Semitism and as something that came between him and his enjoyment of the first Rome, the love object. It had been a symbol to him of all that was inaccessible to the Jews, and he called it "the lie of salvation."

In one of his letters to Fliess, Freud cited a passage from one of the variants of the Oedipus legend:

"The conquest of Rome will fall to the arm of him who should first 'kiss' his mother."

This was a reversal of the idea that in order to sleep with your mother you must first conquer the enemy. Hannibal, a boyhood hero of Freud, had ordered his armies to overcome Rome but they never did; in short, he came close, but failed. Freud, on the other hand, succeeded merely by arriving, thereby fulfilling a wish which till then he had regarded as unattainable. After four years of self-analysis culminating in *The Interpretation of Dreams*, Freud had finally conquered his resistances and could at last realize his triumphal entry.

Freud stands with his brother Alex in the San Pietro in Vincoli, gazing for the first time on Michelangelo's *Moses* (well, mine anyway).

Freud's identification with Moses was strong: he saw himself as the one who would only glimpse the Promised Land of Psychiatry from afar, leaving Jung as Joshua, destined to explore it. It was an image that deeply affected him.

His eyes moistening, he fancied he saw the penetrating eyes of Professor Brücke of the University of Vienna glaring down at him – or were they his father's eyes? Turning to Alex, he inquired:

"By the way, have you been washing your undergarments in the bathroom again?"

At first it is difficult to see why the eyes of Moses (or even Brücke's or his father's eyes, for that matter) should remind Freud of his brother's underwear. Alex is understandably puzzled, until Freud continues:

"Because our cleaning lady gave me some strange looks this morning."

Alex's bewilderment is part of the technique of this joking method, as is the timing of Freud's final remark. It is another **allusion by means of omission joke.**

Ralph STEADman

Freud and his brother Alex enjoy a sedate ride in a horse-drawn cab around the Piazza of St. Peter's in Rome. Relaxed and comfortable, Freud is in high spirits and brightens their tour with a humorous **analogy** about the Church.

"A Catholic cleric behaves rather like a clerk with a post in a large business. The Church, the big wholesale firm whose director is the Pope, gives him a fixed job, for which he receives a fixed salary. He works lazily, as everyone does who is not working for his own profit, for he can easily escape notice in the bustle of the large concern. All he has at heart is the credit of the establishment and still more its maintenance, since if it should go bankrupt he would lose his livelihood.

"A Protestant cleric, on the other hand, is in every case his own principal and carries on the business of religion for his own profit. He does not, like his fellow Catholic traders, carry on a wholesale business but only a retail one. And since he must manage it by himself, he cannot be lazy. He must advertise his articles of faith, he must depreciate his competitor's articles. And, genuine retailer that he is, he will usually be found standing in his retail shop, emanating envy of all the great houses and particularly of the great House of Rome, which pays the wages of thousands of bookkeepers and packers and has its factories in all quarters of the globe."

After riding silently in style for a little while, Alex poses the question:

"I wonder, Sigmund, how many people work in the Vatican?"

"About half of them, I should imagine," replied Freud, smiling as he realized he had just made a **displacement joke.** "At a rough guess," he added— an allusion to the real meaning of Alex's question which, in effect, compounds the division of our train of thought and hence the effect of the joke via a second layer of displacement joking.

Freud was never certain that the type of joke he classified as analogy was, in fact, a pure joking form, as its joking characteristics usually relied on other joking techniques to carry it off. The fact that it is included at all in *Jokes and Their Relation to the Unconscious* must stem from the fact that in the course of an analogy's telling it occasionally gives rise to amusement, though its main purpose must surely be to explain a complicated situation in a commonplace and familiar way.

In 1902 Freud was finally granted the title "Professor Extraordinarius" at the University of Vienna; the appointment came five years after he was first nominated for the post in 1897. The delay was partly due to rampant anti-Semitism in university circles; however, his total preoccupation with self-analysis during his period of "splendid isolation," as he called it, played an equally large role in his persistently being overlooked. When the Emperor Franz Josef finally did confer the professorship on him, Freud was inundated with an avalanche of tributes and congratulations.

Passing the Austrian Parliament on the Ringstrasse in Vienna, he remarked to his colleague and follower Max Graf, using an **analogy:**

"It's as if His Majesty has officially recognized sexuality, the Cabinet has ratified *The Interpretation of Dreams*, and Parliament has passed a bill on the necessity of psychoanalytical therapy in the treatment of hysteria by a two-thirds majority."

As already mentioned, Freud was uncertain as to whether or not analogy was a pure joking form because of its reliance on other joking techniques. The method employed here is **unification** – the making of an unexpected connection to create the joke. Analogous jokes invariably strive to debase by juxtaposing widely different elements. In this case an emperor and his government are mockingly given god-like sanctions over something as basic and undeniable as sexuality.

It is obvious from the remark that, rather than being delighted, Freud was both cynical and bemused by the much-overdue recognition, though it would undoubtedly help his practice and improve his social status: the former meant a lot to him, the latter virtually nothing.

Ralph STEADman 78

It is an evening in 1905, shortly after the publication of Freud's *Three Essays on the Theory of Sexuality*, his most controversial work. The "odious Professor Freud" is taking a stroll along the Kartnerstrasse with "that poor woman," his wife Martha. He is at the height of his productivity and finally emerging, in a scientific sense, from his "splendid isolation" of some ten years. In the eyes of polite Viennese society, not to mention the whole medical profession, he was now considered loathsome, ridiculous and obscene. This was the man who claimed that children were born with sexual urges that every nanny knew about, occasionally excited, but preferably repressed . . .

The "odious Professor Freud" had actually had the audacity to write that, in effect, up to the age of five these urges gradually develop, allowing the child to learn about his erogenous and erotogenetic zones; then, after a latency period, during which much is unlearned or forgotten, the child enters puberty and begins its adult erotic life, during which these urges re-emerge, only this time in the form of fixations, jealousies, hang-ups and so on.

For instance, if the child who is learning to ride a horse notices a pleasurable sensation derived from the rubbing that occurs at the junction of skin in the area of the ano-rectal mucous membrane, then in adult life that person can only achieve full sexual satisfaction with their partner saddled up with a bit between his or her teeth – and going at full gallop.

As people veered away from him in horror in the streets of Vienna, a thought crossed his mind. A muttering, a **representation by something connected** type of joke, a **tendentious joke** that was in no way innocent:

"I think I must remind them of some old friend they used to play with!"

Martha admonished him for even mentioning it:
"Naughty, naughty Sigmund!"*

*My editor, conveniently called Superego for the purposes of this project – i.e., she is there to slam the door on any libidinal impulse (or "creativity" as I prefer to call it) – insisted, in her infinite wisdom, to retain these last few words which, in retrospect, I felt were superfluous, being as I am a stickler for precise, mind-scouring economy in all things. But there you are, you see – you can't win 'em all.

Ralph STEADman

While searching for the Men's Room in the Modern Gallery, Freud happens upon a private showing of two new portraits by the most highly thought-of Viennese artist. The work had been commissioned by two extremely shady but influential businessmen as part of their bid to push their way into society. Just as Freud appeared on the scene, a highly influential art critic was asked what he thought of the pictures. He studied the works for an unduly long time (much to Freud's growing physical discomfort) and then, shaking his head as though there was something amiss, he pointed to the narrow gap between the pictures and spoke quietly:

"But you haven't left much room for Jesus Christ!"

Freud jotted down his assessment as he hurried away on his now desperate search for the Men's Room.

Joke Technique: Representation by something Similar — another form of Analogy

But a few scribbles was all he had time for. Unable to repress his urge any longer, he copied the critic's joke technique by relieving himself in a Grecian urn.

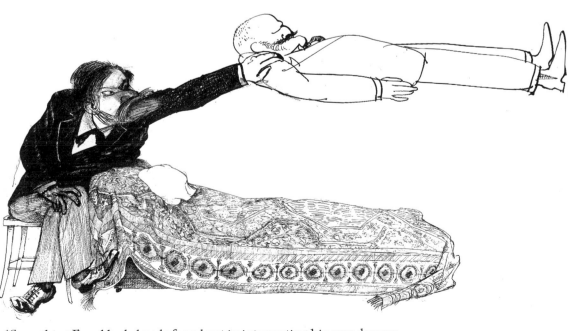

"It remains an uncontradicted fact that if we undo the technique of a joke it disappears."*

*Something Freud had already found out in interpreting his own dreams.

other-watching: Freud at the Burgtheater, enjoying a performance of Sophocles' *Oedipus Rex*, a subject very close to his heart. A lady arrives with her husband and eventually settles herself right in front of Freud, who mutters to himself:

"It is at times like this that even I begin to doubt the soundness of my Oedipus complex."

This is a very mild joke, of course, but one that is full of venom. Flitting across Freud's mind is the thought that if he were Oedipus and this woman, by some weird quirk of Fate, was his mother, he would do her in first, then put the poor wretch sitting next to her out of his misery as an encore. He could then claim, with a typical bit of Jewish *chutzpah*, that he was an orphan who looked upon the stage as a surrogate mother.

This is a situation giving rise to a **tendentious joke** in a category called **condensation with substitution,** which is similar to **allusion by means of modification.** Freud has condensed the psychical effort necessary to appreciate fully his utter frustration by substituting an allusion to a modified interpretation of the Oedipus legend.

Ralph STEADMAN 31. 5.

Read perceiving

Freud's daily walks around the Ringstrasse were frequently enhanced by a leisurely coffee at the Café Landtmann. This day finds him listening in on a conversation which develops into a joke of **apparent logic** – i.e., one which relies on faulty reasoning.

A gentleman orders borscht, but is persuaded by the waiter to try the chicken soup. The lady with him orders pea soup, but the barley soup is recommended instead. When the soup has been eaten, the waiter is summoned:

    "Waiter, that chicken soup was marvelous. Best I ever tasted!"

    "Why didn't you recommend the chicken soup to me?" demanded the lady.

    "You didn't order the borscht!"

Café Landtmann 2 July 1904

As Freud's reputation grew he began to receive patients from abroad, which suggests that they were probably wealthy. This fact did not escape the notice of the Austrian tax authorities, who eventually sent him a letter demanding an account of his earnings during this active period.

Freud read the letter and remarked:

"Hah! At last! The first official recognition of my work."

At first I thought that the joking technique employed here was **displacement,** diverting an idea from one train of thought to another. But there seemed to be something else at work. I knew it couldn't be a **double meaning joke** for that merely relies on the multiple use of the same word, and jokes in this category are usually verbal as opposed to conceptual. Freud's remark was clearly conceptual – that much I did know.

So then I thought, trying hard to employ some of the formidable reasoning which Freud himself employed: OK, so the joke does not rely on one word, nor does it only display division of a train of thought – but what *does* it do? It contains two main elements: namely, a letter from the tax authorities; and the reason for the letter, i.e. the hard-earned health of Freud's business. These two elements come together in Freud's remark, creating a division of our train of thought that produces a third element – namely, a "defense going to meet the aggressor"; a "ready repartee"; or, as Freud would have it, a **unification joke.**

Freud could have said:

"Hah! They have noticed that I have begun to make a profit" – which is no joke at all.

As making money was not the essential reason for Freud's work (though he would be in super tax trouble were he alive today), he throws the troublesome nature of the letter right back at them by relating it to the content of his work (which would have been the last thing on a taxman's mind), thus creating the joke. Good!

The last laugh, however, was still with the Austrian tax authorities.

To Freud, all forms of religious observance were foolish and superstitious. His wife Martha, on the other hand, took religion much more seriously, as her grandfather had been a prominent rabbi in Hamburg. It took Freud many years before he finally managed to persuade her to move away from her strict observance of orthodox Jewish customs. And, indeed, even as late as 1938 they were still carrying on a long-standing humorous-serious battle over the issue.

Here is a typical brisk interchange between them as Freud sits down to dinner one Friday evening, having had a particularly harassed day at the office. Minna Bernays, Freud's sister-in-law, is seated between them. Freud speaks first:

"What the blazes is this?"

"You know perfectly well, dear. It's the Sabbath."

"But I thought we settled this years ago."

"We did, dear. But the children are fascinated and they want us to celebrate it."

"But haven't you explained? – it's merely the survival of some tribal neurosis!"

"Yes, dear."

"One of the many outward signs of a collective superego!"

"I'm sure, dear."

"Obsessional neurosis! Defending the tribe against incestuous wishes and the death wish against their father!"

"We know all that, dear. Now, will you recite the blessings or shall I? The children can't wait to see you castr—er—uh—*cut* the challah. Collectively, that is."

The laconic addition at the end of Martha's last remark is a form of vague defensive **condensation** of all that has come before, bringing all of Freud's pedantic statements back to earth, diffusing the psychic tension and making it possible for everyone present to relax back into normal family discourse. The situation is only a joke when one appreciates all the elements involved – rather as a playwright who is able to develop a remark into a joke by carefully constructing the situation into which he is injecting it. It is not the stuff of stand-up comics.

Freud has just asked the patient on his couch if she is ever troubled by immoral thoughts. The patient replies, quite innocently:

"Not at all, Professor, I rather enjoy them!"

– inadvertently creating a **unification joke,** "a defense going to meet the aggressor" in which she has established an unexpected unity between attack and counter-attack.

The phrasing of Freud's question, incidentally, suggests that he had already realized that his patients were constantly having immoral thoughts. In this instance he merely wished to ascertain whether or not they were causing discomfort. It was this particular quality of Freud's to call a spade a spade – the fact that he was "blessed with a penetrating and surpassing realism," as Earnest [sic] Jones* wrote in his biography – that made him so many enemies. But, more importantly, it was also this which led him to the discovery of the **unconscious,** that beehive of base animal instincts demanding satisfaction and fighting to get out from under the heavy-booted rational mind.

*For Freud at least Ernest, a genuine typo often's Freudian slip.

Freud in a drunken stupor at the Café Greinsteidl near the Hofburg, a favorite meeting place for poets, artists, writers, politicians and other assorted lay-abouts at the turn of the century. He wags a finger at the pianist and declares:

"Young man, do you know you're driving me crazy?"

To which the pianist replies:

"No, but if you can hum it, I can play it."

This appears to be a perfect **double meaning joke,** putting the word *know* to "multiple use" without violating it. But to be truthful, the picture itself is something of a **nonsense joke** (see page 87). Freud did not drink and he hated pianos. So showing him lounging around drinking clubs and requesting songs like "Can't You See Your Mother, Baby, Standing in the Shadows?" is actually quite absurd.

N.B.: Sticklers for historical accuracy would also point out that neither Freud nor pianos were ever seen at the Café Greinsteidl.

Freud, an inveterate collector of jokes, overhears a perfect pun – a **reduction joke,** which in Freud's terminology is a joking technique that takes a word or words back to their original form, a requirement that a pun often fulfills:

BLIND MAN (MEETING A LAME MAN): How are you getting along?"

LAME MAN: "As you *see*, dummkopf!"

The building in the background, incidentally, was the first truly "modern" building in Vienna. It is the Loos Haus – known at the time as "The House without Eyebrows" in the Michaelerplatz, designed by Adolf Loos in 1910 as an austere protest against the Ringstrasse architecture of the Secession movement, which Loos considered degenerate and overly ornamental. Attempting to restore the word Haus to its full meaning, Loos said:

"The Haus has to please everyone to distinguish it from Art – which does not have to please anyone!"

Karl Kraus, satirist and editor/owner of the magazine *Die Fackel*, considered that he was doing for language what Loos was doing for architecture – that is, "making people morally aware of the essential difference between a chamber pot and a Grecian urn."* Kraus developed an aversion to psychoanalysis, which he referred to as "that disease which purports to be the cure." Freud would have seen this as **unification joke,** using an economy of psychical effort which constitutes the essence of true wit.

N.B.: It should be recorded that Karl Kraus noted with unsavory glee the destruction of the Café Greinsteidl (see pages 68-69) in 1904, which subsequently became the site of the Loos Haus. It signified for him the fall of the phony artists and writers who wallowed nauseatingly in the café's soporific decadence – though, no doubt, it would be a great place to go and wallow nauseatingly today, Kraus or no Kraus!

*Cf. pages 52-53 where Freud finds himself in a similar moral dilemma.

Freud overhears a perfect pun —
A Reduction Joke

Blind Man (meeting a Lame man) "How are you getting along?"
Lame Man. "As you see, Dumpkopff!!"

Ralph STEADman 23.5.77

For many years Freud paid daily visits to the little barber in the Schottenpassage for a beard trim. On this occasion we find the barber, an excitable man, gesticulating dangerously with his scissors as he speaks with enthusiasm of his daughter and the fine young man she has been lucky enough to marry. Miraculously, Freud's facial protrusions missed clipping by a hair's breadth. Suddenly he declared:

"Herr Lobner*, I am very happy for you and your daughter's good fortune, but if you are as flamboyant cutting your son-in-law's hair as you are cutting mine, then he may well end up less than you claim him to be."

This is another example of an **allusion by omission joke.** Freud rather delicately omits the thought that fear of castration looms uppermost in his mind at this moment, constituting what he would have called a **real anxiety** (one that is triggered by a clear and present danger), as opposed to a morbid anxiety. A **morbid anxiety** is present when someone fears something in their **id,** or primitive instinctual unconscious – something which they cannot describe. In such cases the id is reprimanded severely by the **superego,** or puritanical conscience, which in turn causes the **ego,** or rational self, a spot of trouble trying to keep the peace. More often than not, morbid anxiety in males is prompted by an unconscious fear of castration. In this instance, however, there is no doubt in Freud's mind that mutilation in one form or another has some foundation and, therefore, we are justified in considering his present anxiety *very* real.

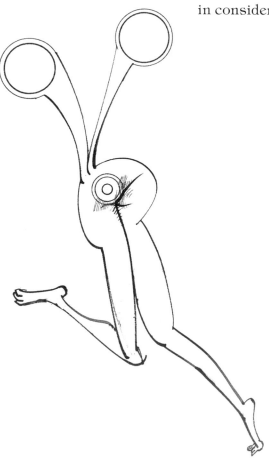

*The real Herr Lobner (Herr Hans Lobner) is not a barber, but is in fact Curator of the Freud Museum in Vienna, to whom I am greatly indebted for his kindness and invaluable help during the course of the book's development and to whom I dedicate this drawing.

Ralph STEADman 78

"The sexual life of man is seriously disabled; it sometimes gives the impression of being a function in process of becoming atrophied."

Civilization and Its Discontents

N.B.: The picture does not require analysis – perhaps the artist does.

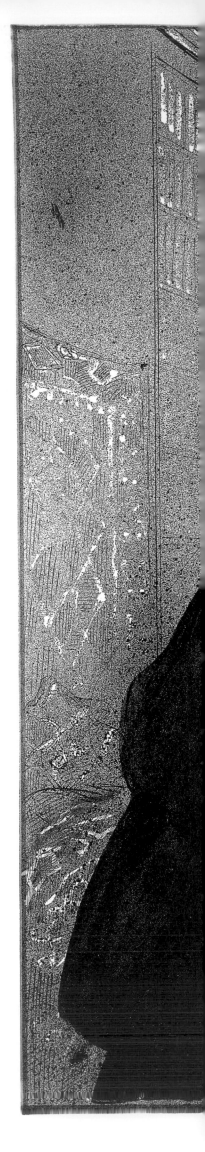

Carl Gustav Jung, a budding young Swiss psychologist and ardent admirer of Freud, first visited him on Sunday, February 27, 1907, at 10 AM. He had so much to tell Freud that he held forth for three hours before Freud himself could get a word in. When he did, he organized (in a fatherly way) all that Jung had said under precise headings so that they might discuss each point in turn.

"**So tell me,**" remarked Freud, obviously impressed. "**What would you say to a partnership in the business?**"

"**Herr Professor,**" replied Jung, like a respectful son, "**I am deeply honored . . . and if it doesn't work out,**" he added, completing the **analogy, "we can always sell bagels!**"

Jung had afforded himself his let-out clause, a gentle anti-Semitic dig in the form of a **tendentious joke.**

Freud was very strict to ensure that his patients arrived for their treatment punctually and that after their session they would not have to leave via the waiting room. They were always shown out by another door, thus avoiding confrontation and possible embarrassment between patients. It was particularly necessary to exercise caution in those early days of psychoanalysis, for anyone even interested in the subject, let alone suspected of being a patient, was regarded with suspicion and contempt.

But it was not always possible to avoid such encounters. Let's say that Freud is having a session with a patient who has a tendency to gossip – for example, the wife of Kaiser Wilhelm II (which would make her Queen Victoria's granddaughter). When the session is over, she leaves by the appropriate exit, only to discover that she has left a glove in the waiting room.

"Leonora!" she exclaims, as she re-enters the waiting room and happens to recognize Leonora de Rothschild, wife of Mayor Alphonse de Rothschild, second-in-command of the Paris family's banking house in Vienna. **"I didn't know you were undergoing psychoanalytical treatment!"**

"Of course, I'm not," snaps Leonora, obviously startled by the last person she wanted to meet in Sigmund Freud's house. **"As a matter of fact, I'm only here to discuss the catering for the B'nai B'rith* meeting next Monday. Professor Frung is giving a lecture."**

"Oh, ho!" replies the other, picking up her glove and leaving triumphantly.

Leonora's classic Freudian slip did not go unnoticed by the Kaiser's wife; it immediately suggested to her that Leonora must have been more familiar with Freud and his work than she was prepared to admit. Her slip of the tongue was a mode of self-betrayal – an expression of something she did not wish to say.

*A Jewish society which Freud belonged to all his life.

Chronic congestion and heavy cigar smoking (twenty a day) were the cause of much hawking and spitting for Freud, which, according to a story fermented by biographer Paul Roazen, he often carried out in front of his patients. If any of them suddenly sat up or displayed any signs of squeamishness, they were severely admonished thus:

"Madam! If you cannot control your reactions, I'll be forced to fart as well, just to prove how lucky you are!"

This is a crude **omission with substitution joke.** What has been omitted has been replaced by an inference which alludes back to what has been omitted – the inference here being Freud's reminder to his patient that there are worse things than hawking and spitting, but good manners prevent him from demonstrating.

N.B.: That Freud did hawk and spit in front of his patients is subject to grave doubt, but that he did bang both his fists on the headpiece of the patient's couch during analysis, for one reason or another, is an indisputable fact.

reud, Jung and Sandor Ferenczi* arriving in New York on Sunday, August 27, 1910, where Jung and Freud have been invited to speak at the twentieth anniversary of Clark University in Worcester, Massachusetts.

Freud had had a fainting fit in Bremen on the evening before their departure for New York, caused perhaps by Jung's persistent talk of corpses, which Freud had interpreted as possibly a death wish which Jung harbored against him. Despite this, the three men spent much of the voyage psychoanalyzing each other's dreams. Freud, however, rarely provided the associations to the dream material he offered, on the grounds that it might undermine his authority as leader of the psychoanalytical movement. According to Jung, he felt particularly inhibited where the material related to the intimate triangle made up of himself, his wife Martha and his sister-in-law, Minna Bernays.

As the boat pulls into New York Harbor, Ferenczi is suddenly compelled to throw up over the side of the ship.
"Ohoooeroh! It must have been something I ate!
Freud turns away squeamishly and whispers:

*Ferenczi was another of Freud's ardent followers. At one point Freud hoped that he would marry one of his daughters.

"Unless it was something he *thought*."

To which Jung replies: "Perhaps it was something he thought he ate."

To which Freud rejoins: "And if he said he thought he ate something and he hadn't?"

"Then he would be sick before he thought he hadn't," Jung retorts.

"But if he hadn't and he found out *before* he was sick?"

"Then he wouldn't be sick!"

"But if he found out before he was sick that he hadn't eaten what he thought he had and, in fact, *had* eaten something that would make him sick, then he *would* be sick whether he thought it or not."

"Not if the thought he had that he hadn't eaten something that would make him sick was strong — then he wouldn't!"

"Of course he would, my dear Jung. There are some things that even the power of thought cannot dissuade!"

"I don't agree," insisted Jung vehemently. And so the conversation continued . . .

This was not the first time that rumblings of dissent had manifested themselves in Freud's more brilliant pupils, notably Jung and Adler; dissension would continue to grow until Adler's breakaway in 1911 and Jung's in 1913.

It ought to be mentioned that a few moments later, even as Ferenczi was heaving a great sigh of relief, both Freud and Jung turned, as if with a single thought, and emptied the contents of their stomachs into the harbor. It must have been the only time the two men were ever in complete agreement.

Freud would have called their collective response an **irony,** which in fact he did not consider a true joke category. (The nearest thing to it is the technique he called **representation by the opposite,** which is a subspecies of the comic.) To quote Freud:

"Irony can only be employed when the other person is prepared to hear the opposite, so that he cannot fail to feel an inclination to contradict."

Which is exactly what transpired when Ferenczi turned and gazed at the two bowed figures on the deck, and declared:

"It must have been something *I* ate!"

A perfect irony!

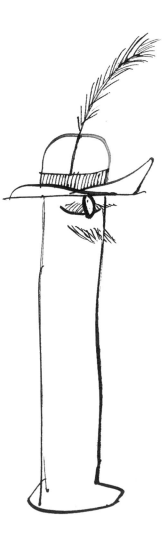

While in New York, Freud, Jung and Ferenczi visited the Lower East Side with their American hosts and fellow psychoanalysts. Abraham Brill was their guide. Though he did not share their orthodox religious beliefs, Freud felt a fierce sense of identification with the Eastern European Jews who by now were well established in the area.

On impulse he bought a new hat from a shop on Hester Street, and in his enthusiasm prompted the rest of his party to do the same. As they left, Freud adjusted his new bonnet and was reminded of an old Jewish joke. Turning to Jung, he sighed:

"Ah! Life is a new hat!"

Jung, looking puzzled and a little awkward in his new tit-fer, asked:

"New hat? Why a new hat?"

And Freud replied:

"How should I know? What am I, a philosopher, too?"

Freud classified this as a **nonsense joke,** a wide category which can employ any of the joking techniques as well as being either **verbal** or **conceptual, innocent** or **tendentious.** To quote Freud (and it makes me feel good to do so):

The nonsense that still remains in a conceptual joke acquires secondarily the function of increasing our attention by bewildering us. It serves as a means of intensifying the effect of a joke, but only when it acts obtrusively so that the bewilderment can hurry ahead of the understanding by a perceptible moment of time.

The joke perplexed Jung, who resolved to try it on Ferenczi. The next morning at breakfast he found his opportunity:

"Ah! Life is a suspension bridge!"

Ferenczi replied without so much as a pause:

"I know, I thought the very same thing as I pulled the plug out of the bath this morning."

Jung's egg fell off his spoon and dripped onto the fob of his watch, where it hung precariously before slithering down the leg of his trousers onto a newly polished shoe.

Wilhelm Stekel, one of the "Big Three" dissenters within the psychoanalytical movement who was noted for his understanding of dream symbolism, was fond of claiming that he had surpassed Freud's success. Though his work contained some bright and fresh ideas, it was subject to wild suppositions of a rather journalistic kind. He was fond of boasting of his superiority over Freud by saying:

"A dwarf on the shoulder of a giant could see farther than the giant himself."

Overhearing this on his way to the lavatory, Freud commented sharply:

"Hmm! that may be true, but a louse on the head of an astronomer does not!"

This is a subspecies of **conceptual joke** known as **representation by something similar,** which is also allied to the category known as **double meaning with allusion.** The word *louse* alludes to a multitude of possible opinions about Stekel

The temptation to practice the new language of psychoanalysis on each other must have been irresistible to one and all during their frequent meetings. Anything from picking hairs off a colleague's lapel to not locking the lavatory door must have provoked analysis and gossip to an unnerving degree, and everyone would have surely been on their sharpest guard to avoid betraying any sign of a pet neurosis.

Stekel's constant assertion that unrestrained masturbation was harmless led many to speculate on what Ernest Jones called "Stekel's troublesome neurotic complaint." Freud treated him for it with complete success, making Stekel one of the few patients, it is said, who responded so successfully to treatment.

The disciples' childish manner and bitchiness at this time were further fueled by Freud's dread of being usurped by one or all of his followers, an anxiety which manifested itself in his insisting that he was the father of the movement and they his children.

Freud later referred to Stekel and Adler (seen in the picture directly above the scowling Freud) as "Max and Maurice" – "the naughtiest and nastiest boys in the world," created by the German cartoonist Wilhelm Busch whom Freud admired. A collection of Busch's work in a large book was always on show in the waiting room adjoining Freud's consulting room.

Ralph STEADman

In Germany the abuse ladled onto Freud for years after the publication of his *Three Essays on the Theory of Sexuality* was not altogether unwelcomed or unexpected by Freud. At least he was no longer treated with indifference; he could now see the enemy.

A fierce critic would not be unlike himself – studious, concerned, self-important, phlegmatic, censorious and, above all, human. Thousands of neurologists, psychiatrists and medical men of the time, still reeling under the effects of Darwin, may have looked like him, talked like him, thought like him and even had the same sort of ideas as him. But invariably they repressed them, turning any objectivity they might have had into rancor and embittered pack howling.

Suddenly this upstart – a Jew, no less – was claiming that sexuality was the source of hysteria; that dreams contained the psychology of neurosis in a nutshell; and that when related, they could provide the scientific data needed to penetrate an individual's neurotic symptoms. And, as if that weren't enough, now they were being told that babies, scarcely out of the womb, were pleasurably motivated by erotic impulses in order to survive. The idea proved too much for most to digest, and yet many (if not most) of his detractors must have harbored a wistful identification with such notoriety, sensing "There but for me go I." Yet still they screamed with self-righteous indignation. As Ferenczi himself pointed out:

"If the opponents denied Freud's theories, they certainly dreamed them."

But self-righteous indignation need not be without its own jokes. Here we have Professor Wilhelm Weygandt, a German neurologist and psychiatrist, banging his fist on the lectern at a congress in Hamburg in 1910, and shouting:

"This is not a topic for discussion at a scientific meeting. This is a matter for the police!"

This is a **unification joke with a tendency toward overstatement.** Weygandt's attitudes are made clear by the juxtaposition of three elements: (a) the topic, i.e., psychoanalysis;

(b) the question of its discussion at a congress; and (c) the expression of the congress's consensus of opinion in the form of an overstatement, which serves to underline their objection to Freud's work by suggesting that it be criminally investigated, rather than scientifically discussed.

On the same occasion Professor Weygandt, airing his opinions on psychoanalysts as sexually perverted psychopaths, is said to have uttered the following gem:

"Freud's method of treatment is on a par with massage of the genital organs!"

This is another example of **analogy,** that broad "doubtful" category of joking method in which the triggering of laughter depends solely on the choice of simile or metaphor that constitutes the basis of the joke. The professor's choice here is a dangerous one. It is doubtful that anyone would have dared to laugh at such a remark for fear of displaying the merest sneaking regard for the enemy camp. This was certainly neither the time nor the place for levity.

iking in the woods gave Freud a great deal of pleasure, whether he was alone or with family and friends. He was brisk and tireless. And though he suffered from fears of dying at an early age (fifty-one, he reckoned, based on one of Fliess's periodic laws) and showed psychoneurotic symptoms of heart disease, some of which were attributed to nicotine poisoning, he was undoubtedly a man of robust health.

At the height of his creative powers, he displayed supreme confidence in himself and his work; and in spite of the dissension among his followers he continued to do so. His mother's love for him was immense, and he was secure and happy in the knowledge of it: from it sprang his indomitable courage and single-minded purpose. From where he stood on the Leopoldsberg in the Wienerwald, he looked down on the city that had nurtured his ideas and yet rejected his most unsavory findings and mused:

"My God, Mother, what a sight! From

Ralph STEADman

here on a clear day one can almost see one's opponents fighting tooth and nail among themselves."*

Nothing Freud ever said, did or thought was very far from the central ferment that ruled his every waking hour. In fact, at the very pinnacle of achievement, every human soul – no matter how great or small – continues to be irritated by the very doubt that began the relentless process of searching creativity in the first place.

The International Psychoanalytical Association held its third and one of its most successful congresses in Weimar in September 1911. Although notes of dissent within the movement had been evident for some time (Adler had already resigned from the association), Freud and Jung were still on the best of terms and everyone was in a jovial mood.

Throughout the congress Jung had been making some rather coarse jokes, which Freud considered quite healthy as they provided light relief between sessions of discussion. During one of these interludes, however, someone seemed to have perpetrated something a little coarser. Freud glared at Jung and demanded:

"Damn it, man! Have you just farted?"

To which Jung replied:

"Of course I have. Do you think I *always* smell like this?"

If he were not so taken aback (by the answer as well as by the pervading imposition on the atmosphere), Freud might have identified this technique of joking as **representation by the opposite,** in which the replacement of the really appropriate denial of an embarrassing occurrence with a firm "Yes" has served to diffuse the ticklish moment. If someone other than Jung were involved, Freud might also have classified

*A highly **tendentious joke** in the **displacement** category.

the joke as **obscene,** a category which takes in both sexual and excremental jokes.* Freud considered such jokes to have techniques which were quite wretched in spite of their immense success in provoking laughter. Jung, of course, was incapable of displaying wretched techniques in any sphere.

Incidentally, if one must be wretched (and I can't help myself at times), it is worth considering that if Freud had said:**"Damn it, man. You just farted in front of Lou Andreas-Salomé"** and Jung had replied: **"I do apologize, old chap. I didn't realize it was her turn!"** – it would have created a **smutty joke** using the **double meaning technique,** putting the phrase *in front of* to multiple use without violating the phrase.

Present in the picture from left to right are: Otto Rank, Sandor Ferenczi, Freud, Max Eitingen, Ernest Jones, Carl Jung, Karl Abraham, Ludwig Binswanger, Wilhelm Stekel, Lou Andreas-Salomé, James J. Putnam and Abraham Brill. The culprit, by the way, was Ernest Jones, who was always a very quiet person.

*For a brief overview of Freud's views on **obscene jokes,** see page 22. Freud wrote that:

Smut is originally directed toward women and may be equated with attempts at seduction. . . . Sexual material which forms the content of smut includes more than that which is peculiar to each sex; it also includes that which is common to both sexes and that to which a feeling of shame extends – that is to say, that which is excremental in the most comprehensive sense. This is, however, the sense covered by sexuality in childhood, a time when things sexual and excremental are barely, if at all, distinguished.

Phobias are physical manifestations of neurotic symptoms. It is impossible to know every phobia and, indeed, new phobias spring up in each new age and in each new situation that one finds oneself in.

The common ones – **claustrophobia** (fear of confined spaces), **acrophobia** (heights), **entomophobia** (insects), **equinophobia** (horses), **cynophobia** (dogs), **demonophobia** (witches), **brontophobia** and **astraphobia** (thunder and lightning), **aquaphobia** (water) and many others, including even **pantophobia** (fear of everything) – were difficult enough to trace the sources of. But matters were made still more complex when Freud discovered that some patients even suffered from **Freudrophobia.** It took all the jokes Freud had at his disposal to dispel such fears, particularly when these fears arose from a patient's realization of what he might reveal during the course of psychoanalysis.

Imagine a patient arriving at Freud's consulting room at 19 Berggasse after suffering a desperate journey in the grip of **agoraphobia** (a morbid fear of public places). He reels back as he is seized by an attack of

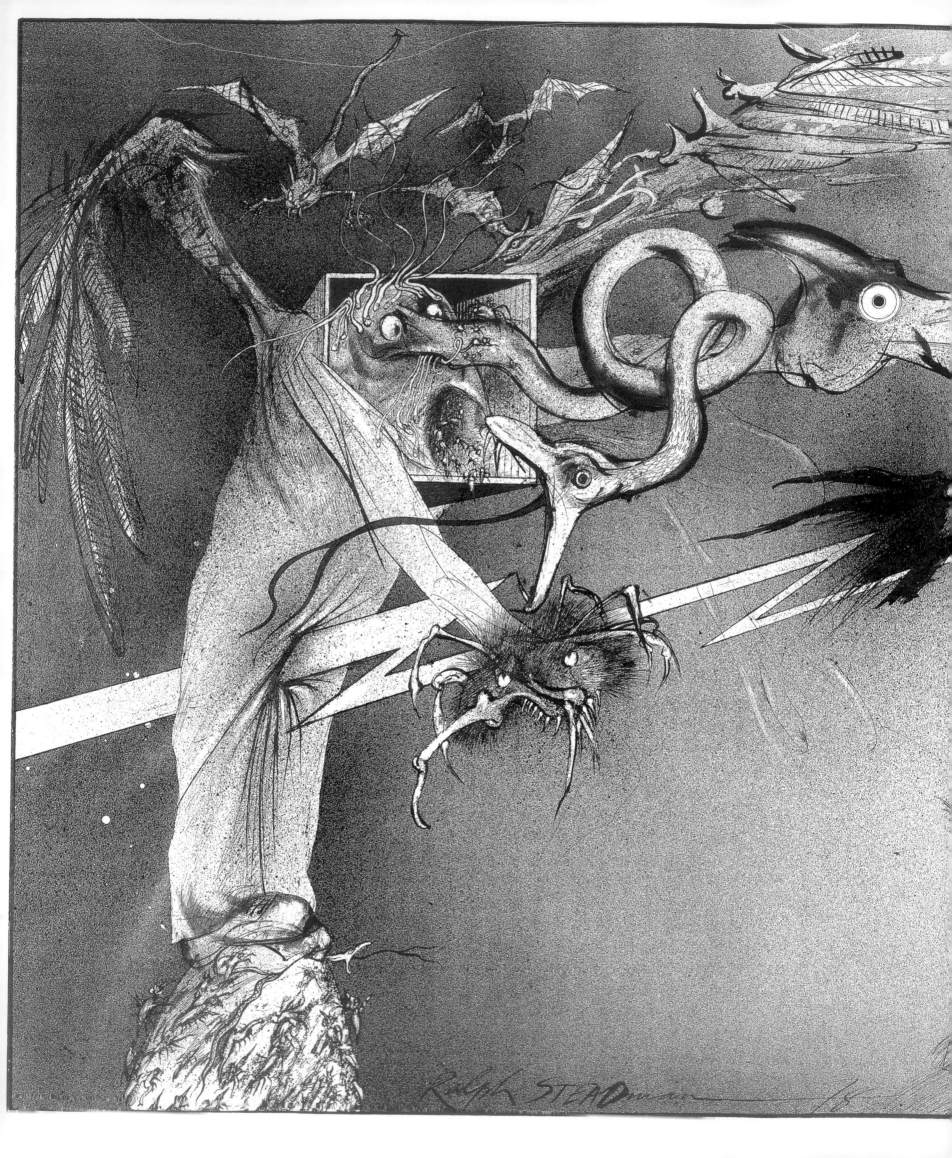

Ralph STEADMAN

architombraphobia (fear of collapsing buildings). Freud is already at the door, intent as he always was on getting his patients to be punctual by instilling in them **tardrophobia** (fear of being late). With a wave of his cigar – for he always had one, suffering as he did from **fumophobia** (fear of being without one) – he invites the desperate figure into his home and reassures him with some wry comment like:

"Why not tie the horse up outside. He'll never make it up the stairs."

This is an **overstatement joke,** in which Freud, while alluding to a horse, is, in fact, denying its existence. He is also attempting to dispel the patient's fear, which the patient may hopefully realize is as ridiculous as the joke.

It might also be mentioned that the situation is an allusion to the case of Little Hands.*

*__The case of Little Hands:__This is a Freudian slip introduced by the manuscript typist, which I have chosen to retain in the finished book. For "Hands" read "Hans," the little boy who suffered a morbid fear of horses, related to the latent hatred and/or penis envy he felt for his father (less well endowed, of course, than a horse) and the seeds of neurosis sown within him when his mother remarked:

"If you do that, I shall send for Dr. A to cut off your widdler. And then what'll you widdle with?"

Never at a loss for words, Hans had retorted: **"With my bottom!"** – a joke of some sort which I'll leave readers to figure out for themselves.

This statue of ladies and gentlemen languishing in their own pendulous prowess does not exist as such in the gardens of the Schloss Schönbrunn, the one-time imperial summer palace of the Hapsburgs. In fact, it does not exist at all. It is the cumulative impression left on the mind of anyone who has paid more than a fleeting visit to Vienna – "City of My Dreams," as some euphoric romantic chose to call it – the legacy of a city's preoccupation with the past glories of the Austro-Hungarian Empire. The nubile expressionism rampant in the statues throughout the city is imbued with the authority of the State and serves as a safety valve of sorts for the frustrations of a hypocritical society.

The duplicity of Viennese life in Freud's time was amply personified in the grandiose rippling vulgarity of the art displayed in public areas. In the minds of the wives of bourgeois society at the turn of the century, sexual enjoyment could only be equated with lewdness, depravity and fallen women. If they experienced any enjoyment at all of the sex act within their marriages, hysterical guilt feelings plagued their minds.

Husbands, however, could find their sexual gratification in the dark, underground, illegal world of the prostitute. In spite of the apparent imperial splendor of the city after the fall of the Hapsburg Empire in 1918, Vienna was a seething mass of poverty, overcrowding and covert sexual activity in all its multifarious combinations – a phenomenon observed and written about by men like Arthur Schnitzler, Karl Kraus and Stefan Zweig in their own enlightened ways and seen by their young contemporary, Adolf Hitler, through the grimy window of his own sexual problems, as a melting pot for blood defilement and venereal disease in which the Jews were the ultimate arch culprits.

"How towns love to hide under clean busy streets and elegant promenades, the subterranean canals of the filthy sewers where the sexual life of the young is supposed to take place invisibly," remarked Arthur Schnitzler to Freud as they walked across the Schönbrunn Gardens one somber Viennese day.

There was a pregnant silence.

"Did you just make that up?" asked Freud somewhat at a disadvantage, having not yet read Stefan Zweig's impressions of Vienna.

"By the way," he countered, grandiloquently, **"did I tell you? My daughter Sophie's getting married!"**

After the First World War, life in Vienna, as in the rest of Europe, was hard and harrowing. Inflation and the simultaneous collapse of the Austro-Hungarian Empire rendered many people's savings worthless, including Freud's. Things would never be the same again. The Russian Revolution, the doctrine of self-determination and people's realization of their own collective power saw to that.

Freud had to face up to the reality that local patients could no longer afford to pay for psychoanalysis, no matter how mad they might be. Now even cigars, Freud's favorite vice, were in short supply, and throughout the two bitter winters immediately following the war he had to work dressed in a heavy overcoat. Add to this the preceding years of disappointment, the betrayal and bickering of old friends and colleagues, the dissension of important followers like Jung and Adler and, even more poignantly, the untimely death of his daughter Sophie at the age of 27 in 1920, and it is not difficult to see why Freud might have thought that he ought to take Misery itself onto his couch as a suitable client for treatment.

It might be pointed out that nobody ever undergoes psychoanalytic treatment because he is happy, except possibly those intent on becoming analysts themselves. Spare a thought, then, for the analyst who sits day after day listening to the desperate outpourings of fractured minds. Albeit a chosen profession, the analyst nevertheless requires a pretty strong constitution to endure it, and there is always the danger that the **transference process*** will operate from analyst to patient rather than the other way around. The **talking cure** (see page 34) cannot be wholly one-sided, and it is the measure of an analyst's detachment that he be able to assess his own degree of personal involvement and concern. A psycho-analyst's personal problems are often the very reason for his interest in the subject in the first place – just as it was Freud's own deep-seated

***Transference process:** the emotional attachment the patient develops for his analyst; a necessary stage in psychoanalysis. When the transference is resolved, the analyst is perceived as a real object rather than a love object to whom the patient unburdens all the experiences he has previously endured.

problems that provided the necessary driving force for the discovery of psychoanalysis. The fact that several early analysts, like Victor Tausk and Herbert Silberer, ended their own lives tragically, as well as the obvious in-fighting, bitter jealousy and petty childish wrangling that persisted throughout the early days of the movement indicates in no small degree the unhappiness and instability of its adherents.

The last sixteen years of Freud's life were to be his most heroic, apart perhaps from the four years he had spent in self-analysis. He was now at a crucial turning point. In 1923 he discovered that he had cancer of the jaw; he was deeply affected by the death of his Sophie's youngest son, only four years of age. Bitterness was beginning to set in.

But through it all, Freud never lost his sense of humor. Heinrich Heine's remark:

"One must forgive one's enemies, but not before they have hanged!"

– was one he often savored at this time. It was a highly **tendentious joke,** employing a technique that Freud called **apparent logic** – i.e., one that employs faulty reasoning, in this case to hide the fact that the act of "forgiving" is only a pretense.

Though no overt aggression is shown, apparent logic enables the joke teller to be hostile while bribing the hearer with the joke's yield of pleasure into taking sides with him "without any very close investigation." It brings to mind two very similar, though far more malevolent remarks of particularly serious and hostile intent:

"The only good Jew is a dead Jew!" as Goebbels once said, and

"Everytime I hear the word _intellectual_ I reach for my revolver!"

… which was uttered by Goering. The first makes me shudder for obvious reasons; the second makes me laugh – not because I particularly like the man or the all-too-literal intention behind his words, but presumably because I, too, at times harbor some sense of inferiority (and, therefore, hostility) when in the presence of some superior intellect, for fear that this intellect may be used against me.

"What progress we are making. In the Middle Ages they would have burned me. Nowadays they are content with burning my books," wrote Freud to Ernest Jones when his books were publicly burned in Berlin in 1933.

He was using the joking technique he called **allusion.** Freud had long since accepted the way of the world and its attitude to him and his ideas. He knew he was another important link in the long line of heretics from Copernicus to Darwin. The remark might have raised a wry smile from Jones at the time, but it was too highly charged with emotion and significance to be taken lightly.

"Allusion," wrote Freud, **"is perhaps the commonest and most easily manageable method of joking and is at the bottom of the majority of short-lived jokes which will not bear being uprooted from their original soil and kept in isolation."**

In likening himself to a heretic who would normally be burned at the stake, Freud was not only alluding to the world's stock reaction to new ideas in a historical sense, but also surely to his painful awareness of the rise of anti-Semitism in Europe, his observance of it throughout his life in Vienna and the very

history of the Jewish people over four thousand years, not to mention his identification with it.

Actually, the remark makes use of a subspecies of allusion called **indirect representation** – i.e., **representation by something similar.** While the remark is an attempt to remain aloof from the antics of mankind, the bitterness he felt is apparent and far less objective than it was, for instance, in the words he wrote to Lou Andreas-Salomé in 1915 expressing his anxiety about the inevitable estrangement of his followers during the war years:

> **I cannot be an optimist, and I believe I differ from the pessimists only in that wicked, stupid senseless things don't upset me; I have accepted them from the beginning as part of what the world is made of.**

In 1928 a former student of psychoanalysis named Charles Maylan wrote a book entitled *Freud's Tragic Complex: An Analysis of Psychoanalysis*, which used psychoanalytical theory to attack psychoanalysis itself. Unamused, Freud remarked:

"I taught him how to speak and all he can do is swear."

It was a stinging **tendentious joke,** the kind at which Freud was a master. Using the joking technique **overstatement,** he accepts Maylan's knowledge which he himself imparted to him, but resents the man's improper use of it. It is the riposte of a man still very much in combat – a case of a definite followed by an overstated "No."

If an opponent of psychoanalysis had made the remark, he might have put it thus:

"Freud may have taught Maylan how to speak, but only now is he beginning to sing!"

Despite appearances, Freud did manage to retain a sense of humor about some people's derogatory remarks about his work – for instance, the time when his London publisher Leonard Woolf, husband of Virginia Woolf, showed him a cutting from a London newspaper after Freud had fled to the city in June 1938. It was a report on a trial, which highly amused Freud. The plaintiff had stolen a book of Freud's from a large bookstall and the judge had sentenced him to three months in jail:

"I only wish I could sentence you to read all of Freud's books!"

– a perfect **unification joke** in which the displacement of our train of thought is effected by the immediate thought of punishment and its connection with reading Freud's work.

Freud was given his first chow dog in 1928, and though he had not had much contact with animals until then he shared a passion for them with Marie-Bonaparte, Princess George of Greece, who had been a student of his and had become a close friend of the family and of psychoanalysis.

In a letter to the Princess in 1934 he nauseatingly eulogizes on the subject (up to this point I had regarded Freud with nothing less than total reverence!):

> **It really explains why one can love an animal ... with such extraordinary intensity; affection without ambivalence, the simplicity of a life free from the almost unbearable conflict of civilization, the beauty of an existence complete in itself. And yet despite all divergence in the organic development, there is that feeling of an intimate affinity, of an undisputed solidarity. Often when stroking Jo-fi I have caught myself humming a melody which, un-musical as I am, I can't help recognizing as the aria from _Don Giovanni_: "a bond of friendship unites us both."**

It is difficult to make out what his brother Alex is saying in the picture, but I think we can safely label this a **tendentious joke,** or, more precisely, a **smutty joke** using the joking technique of indirect representation that Freud called **allusion by omission.** It is possible to trace the path backwards through a series of easily established associations and inferences, and allude to a hostile attitude that Alex is probably expressing at this moment, while Freud sits enjoying the sunshine and the company of his dog in the garden of his summer residence outside Vienna.

*F*reud being met in Paris by Marie-Bonaparte and William Bullit, the American Ambassador, after fleeing Vienna with his family in June 1938, three months after the Nazi invasion of Austria.

The final fifteen months of his life were spent in London. The cancer in his jaw had reached a horrendous stage. Even his favorite chow dog was repelled by the smell of the putrefying flesh. Freud's reluctance to take drugs did not ease matters:

"I prefer to think in torment rather than not to be able to think clearly."

Finally the agony overcame him. He died on September 23, 1939, at the age of eighty-three, with the help of one-third of a grain of morphia administered by his personal physician . . .

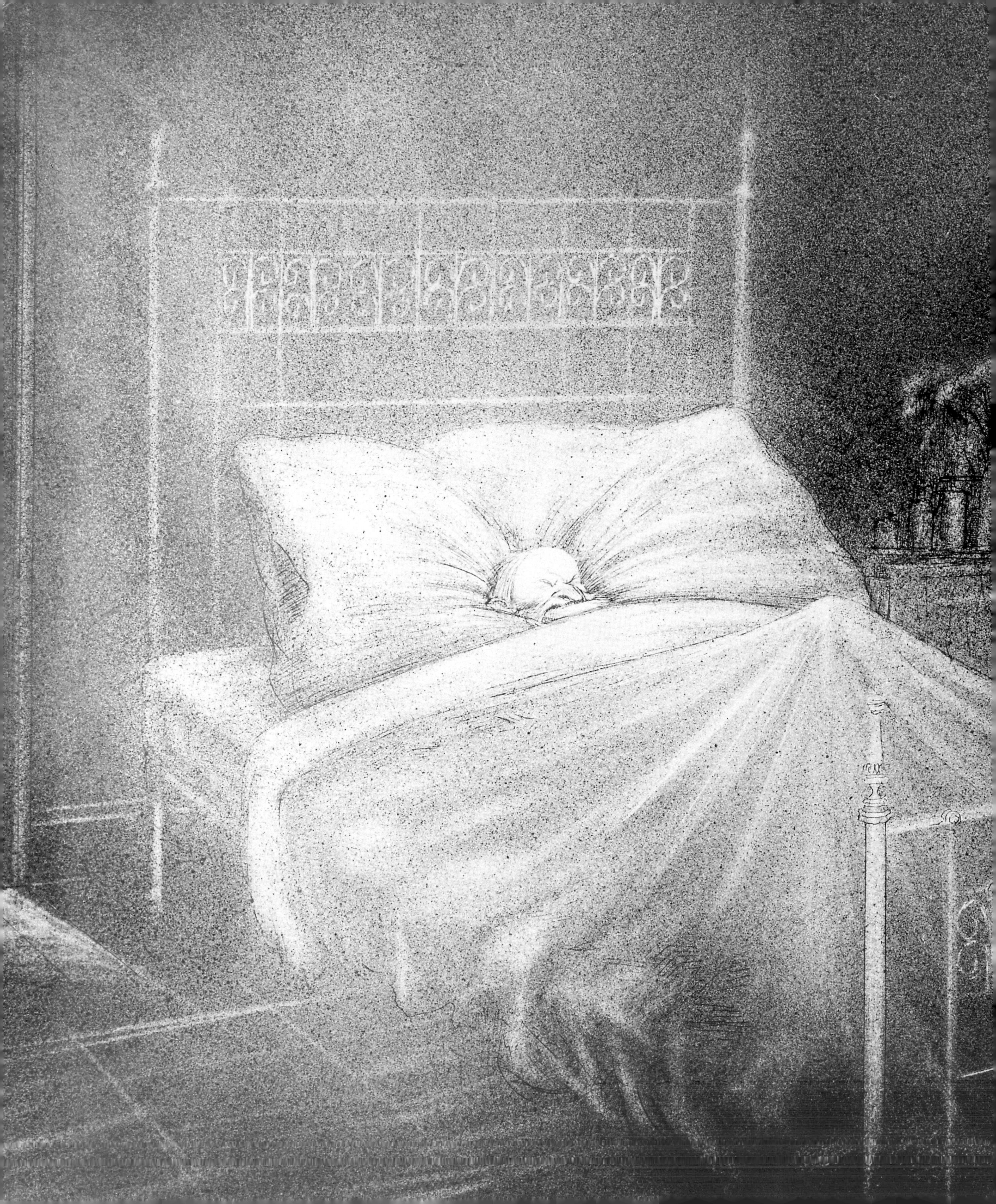

Terms in boldface indicate joking categories and techniques discussed by Freud in <u>Jokes and Their Relation to the Unconscious</u>.

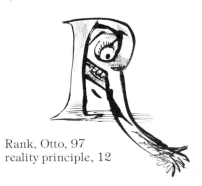